ART
FROM 8 SIMPLE GEOMETRIC
SHAPES

ROSA M.CURTO

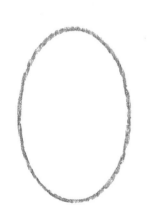   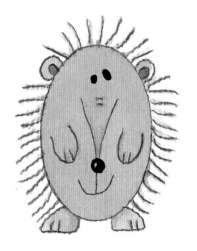

DOVER PUBLICATIONS, INC.
MINEOLA, NEW YORK

SUMMARY

Lots of ideas with 8 geometric shapes

Half circle, 6

Circle, 16

Half oval, 36

Oval, 48

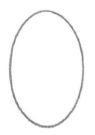    

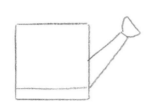

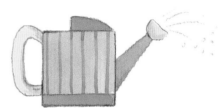

Turning the shapes

Half turn!

You can draw the same shape in two, or even more, positions. Here are a few examples, and you'll find many more as you keep turning the pages.

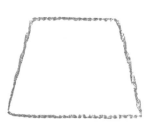

Let's try
a quarter turn!

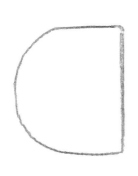

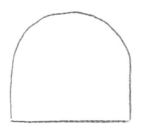

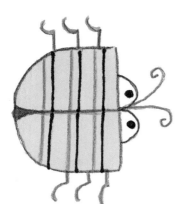

Half circle

1

2

3

4

A slice of
watermelon

A boat

1

2

3

4

A coffee mug

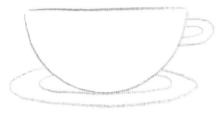 

And... half turn!

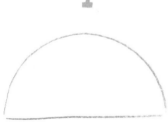

A girl's hat

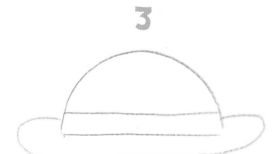 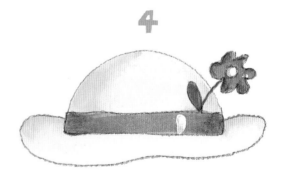

Put it
on its end

The waning moon

1

2

3

4

5

A mushroom

1

2

3

4

5

8

A flower

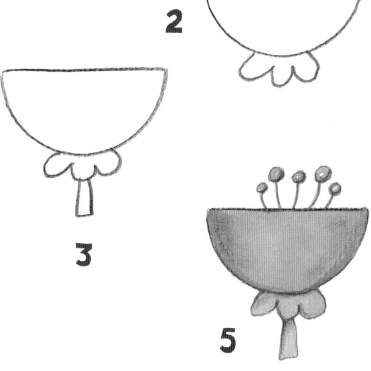

3

4

5

A slice of lemon

1

2

3

4

5

Now, in 6 steps

A basket of fruit

1

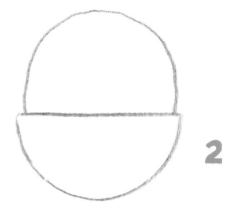

2

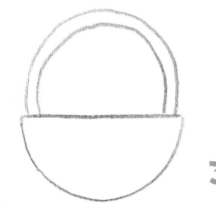

3

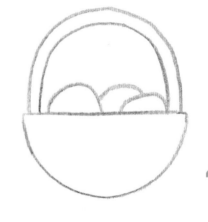

4

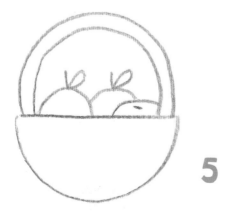

5

6

1

2

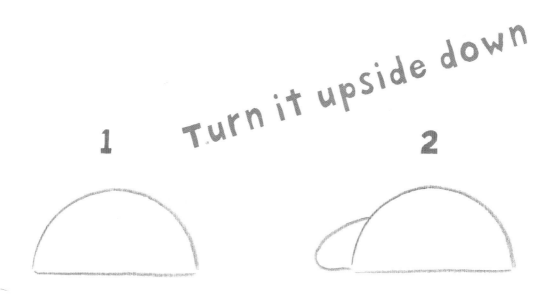

A ladybug

3

4

To draw the ladybug's wings,
draw a curved line on her body.
Did you know all insects have six legs?

5

6

1

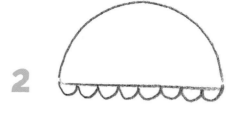

2

Let's go! 7 steps

3

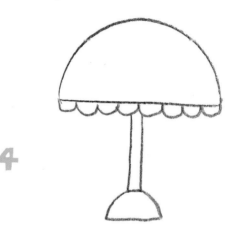

4

A table lamp

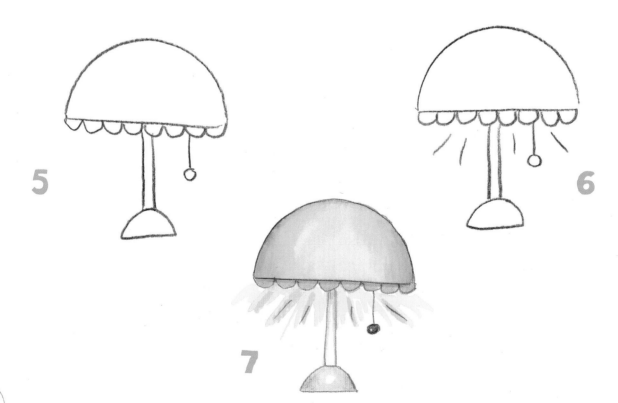

5

6

7

A whale

If you want your whale to look like it's in the water,
add some wiggly lines below the body.

A chicken

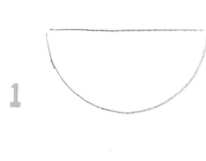

1

2

3

4

can we do it in 8 steps?

5

6

7

8

A car

1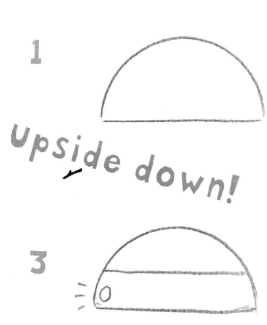

Upside down!

2

3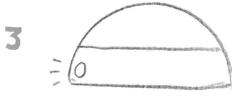

4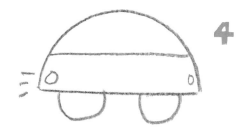

5

6

7

8

15

Circle

A cherry

1 2 3 4

A Christmas ornament

1 2 3 4

A balloon

1 2 3 4

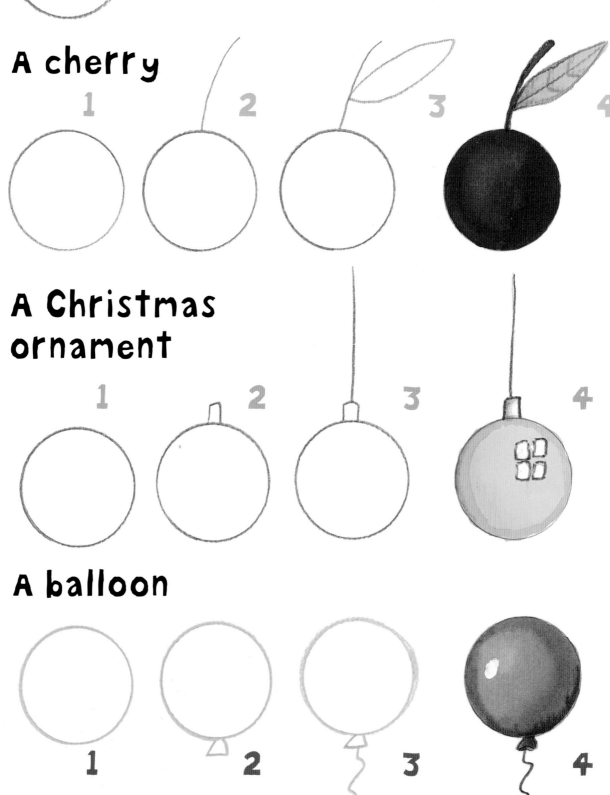

An apple

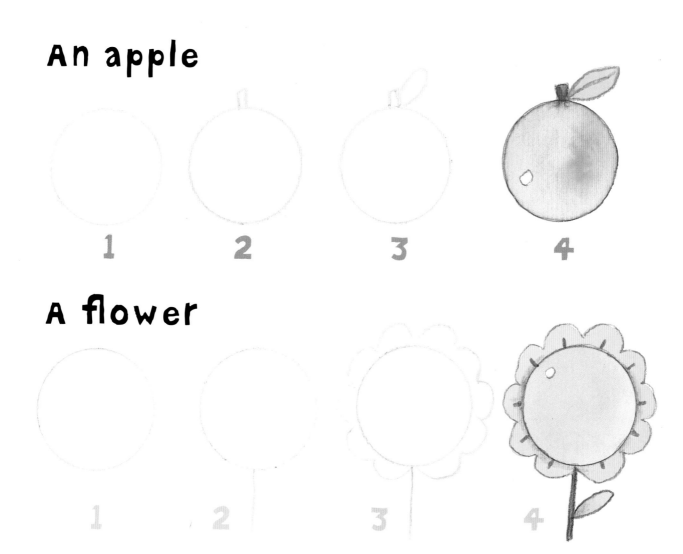

1   2   3   4

A flower

1   2   3   4

Nature is full of round shapes.
Look around and try to spot some more.

An orange

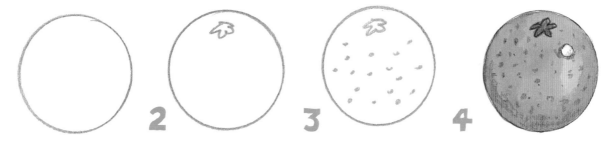

1   2   3   4

A ball

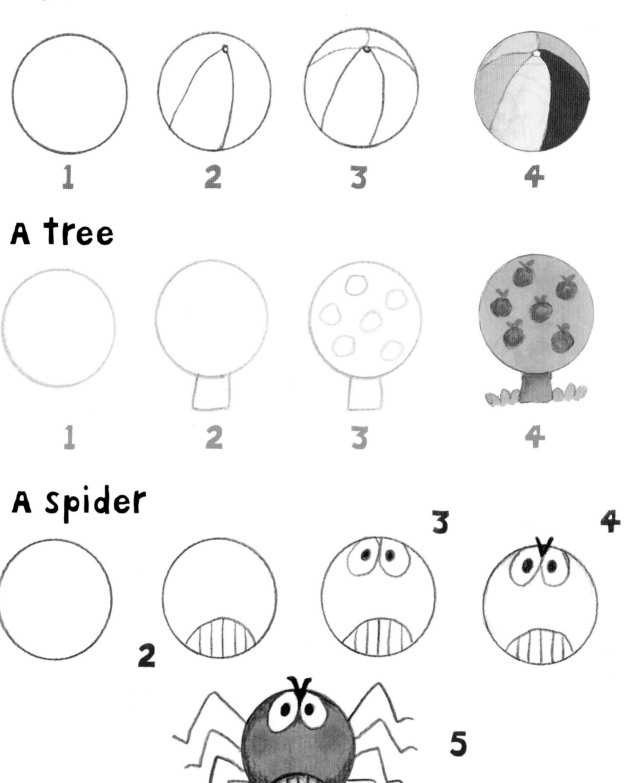

A tree

A spider

The Sun

1   2   3   4

5

Look at how many ways you can draw the Sun.
Try to invent one more!

Happy

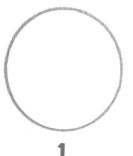

1

2

3

4

5

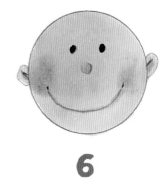

6

Sad

1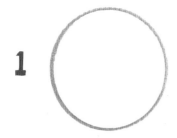

2

3

 4

 5

 6

20

calm

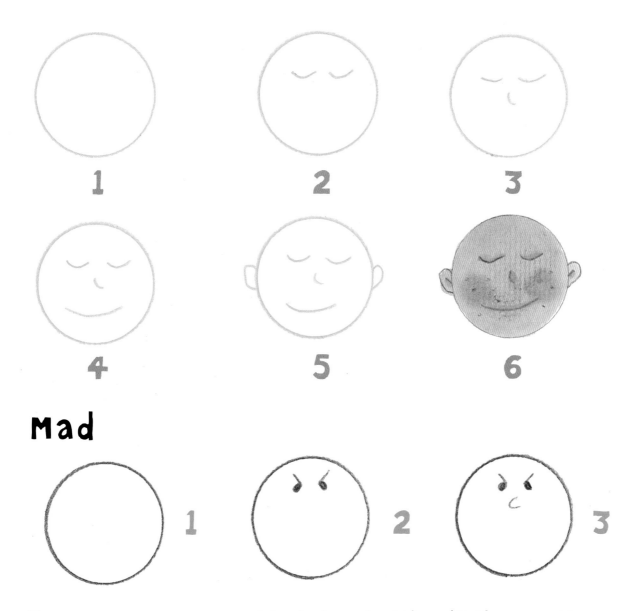

1   **2**   **3**

4   **5**   **6**

Mad

Expressing your mood isn't hard with a little practice.
Give it a try!

Funny faces

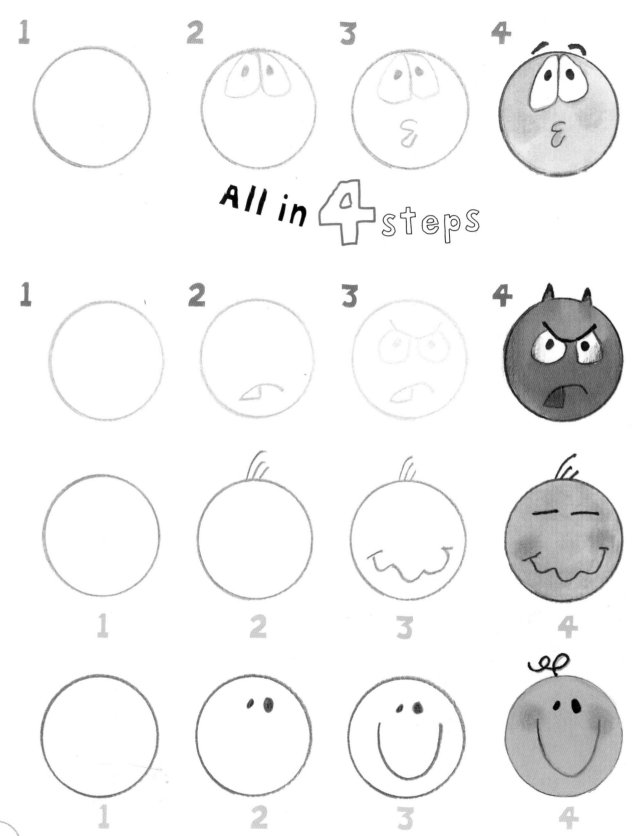

All in 4 steps

1 2 3 4

1 2 3 4

1 **2** **3** **4**

1 **2** **3** **4**

A bunch of round heads

Which one looks most like you?

It's your turn! What other heads did you think up?

Accessories give your character a lot of personality, so try adding different hats, scarves, glasses...

A hot-air balloon

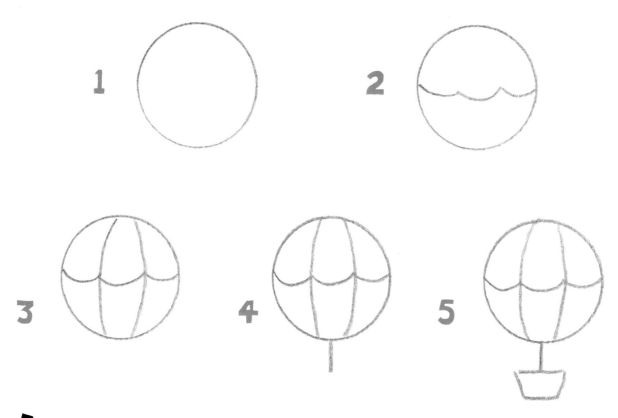

1
2
3
4
5

Easy, in just **7** steps

6

7

A caterpillar

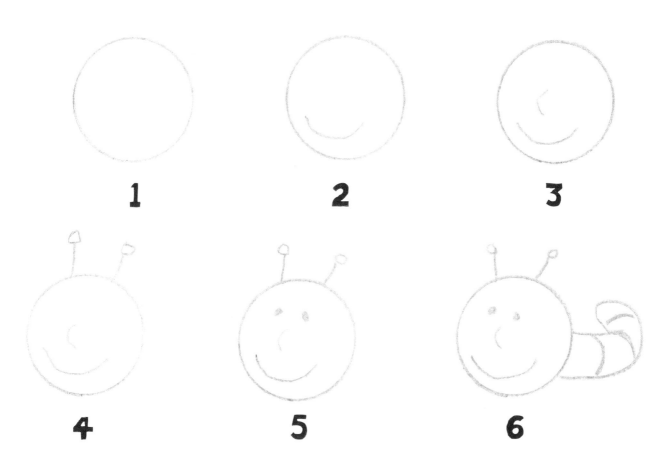

1

2

3

4

5

6

How many circles do you see on our caterpillar?
Don't forget its rosy cheeks!

7

A cat

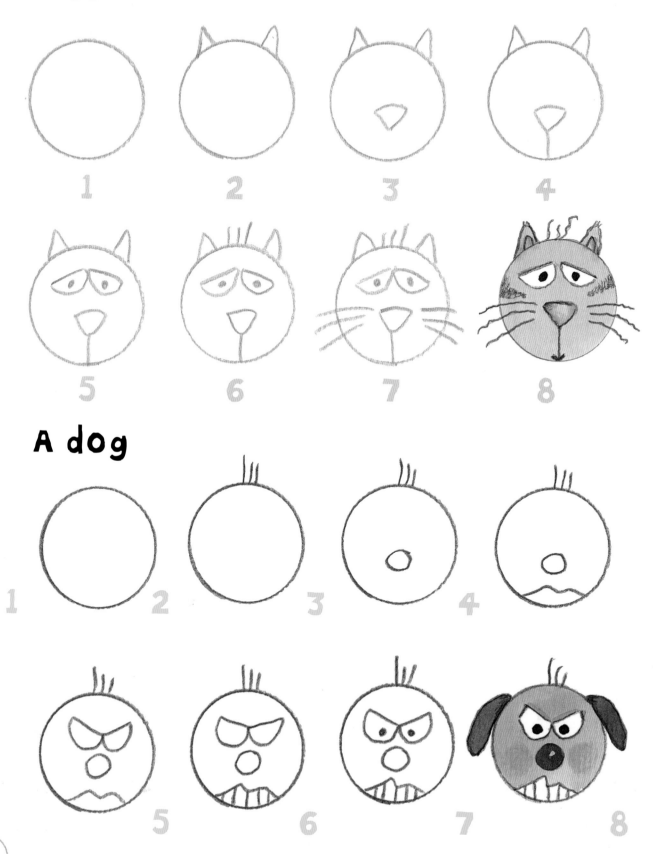

A dog

A bear

1 2 3 4

5 6 7 8

A rabbit

1 2 3 4

5 6 7 8

Some more animals

1

2

3

A bird
on a branch

4

5

6

7

A bat

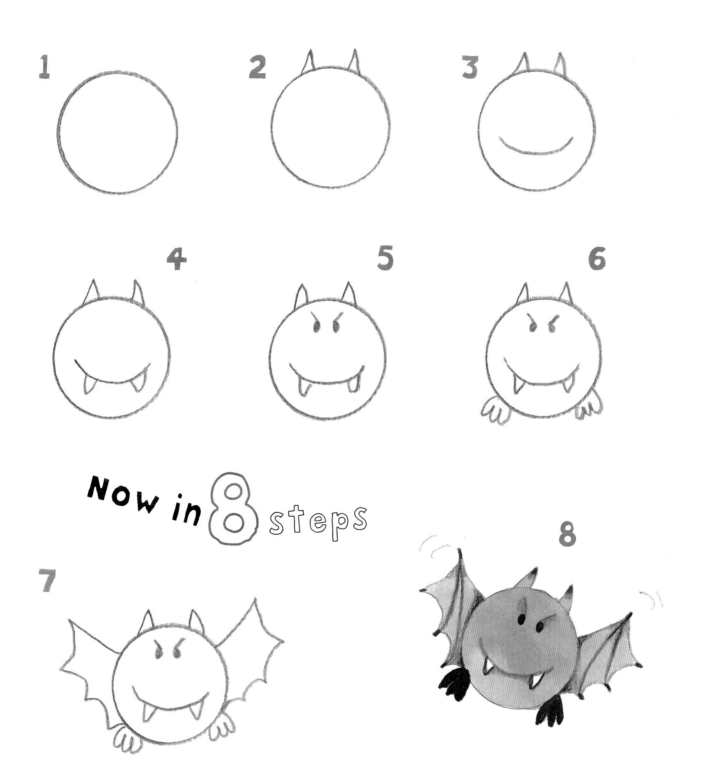

1

2

3

4

5

6

Now in **8** steps

7

8

Let's go! 9 steps

1

2

3

A snail

4

5

6

To make the snail's home,
just draw a spiral inside the circle.

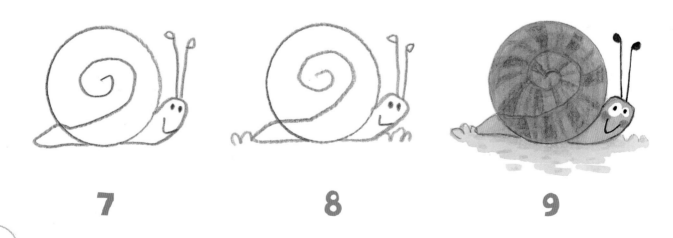

7

8

9

An alarm clock

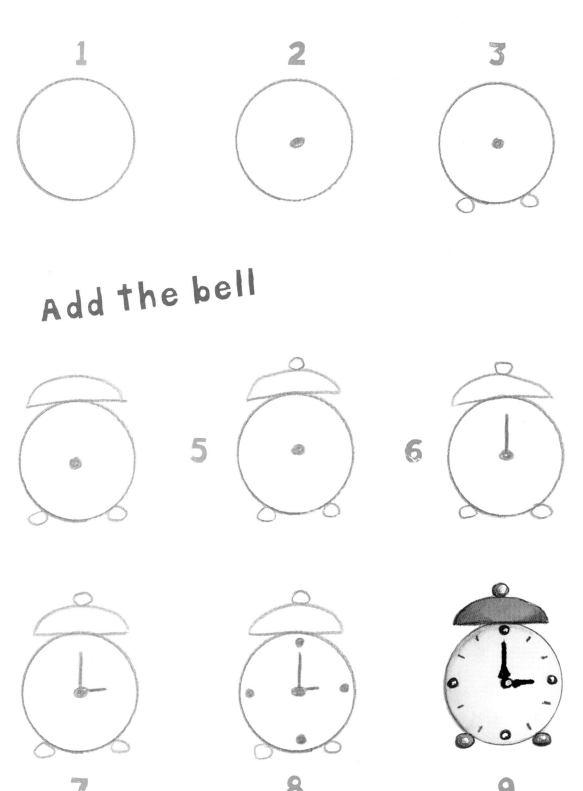

1
2
3

Add the bell

4
5
6

7
8
9

A fish

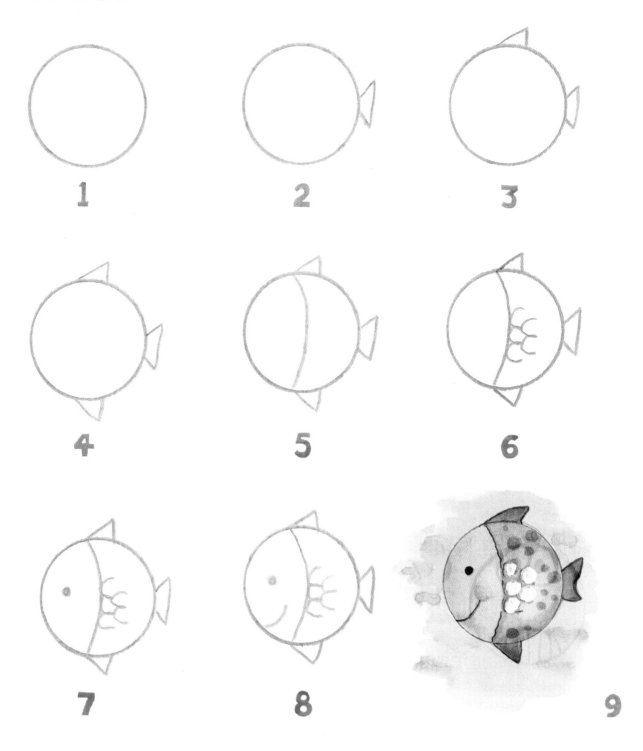

1

2

3

4

5

6

7

8

9

Draw some little bubbles of air with small circles.

A dragon

Try it now with
a dinosaur

Half oval

A jellyfish

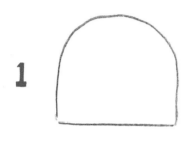 **1**

 **2**

3

4

So easy in 4 steps

1

2

A little cake

3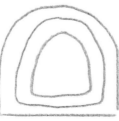

4

A wool cap

A bell

Personalize your creations by coloring them with your favorite colors.

A beetle

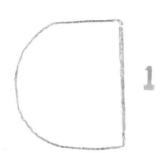 1

 2

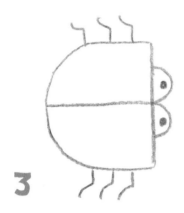 3

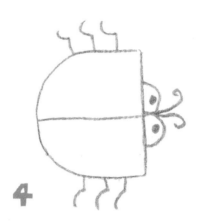 4

5

A lamp

1

2

3

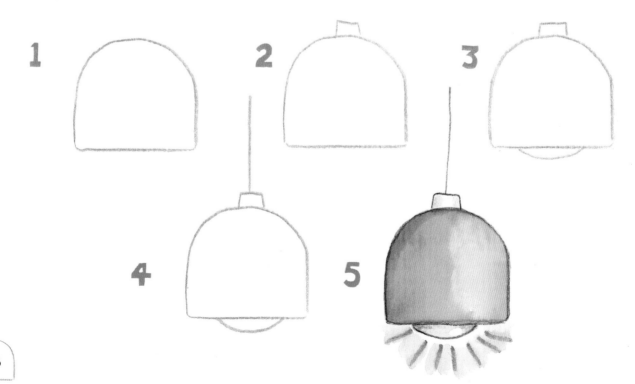

4

5

38

An igloo

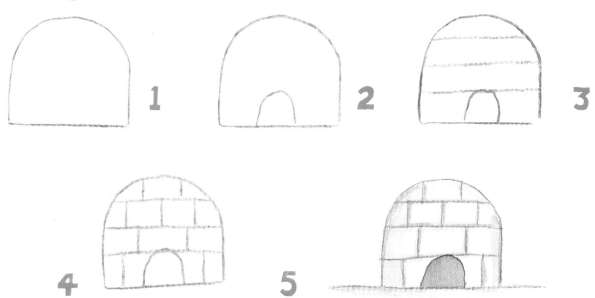

A strainer

And... half turn!

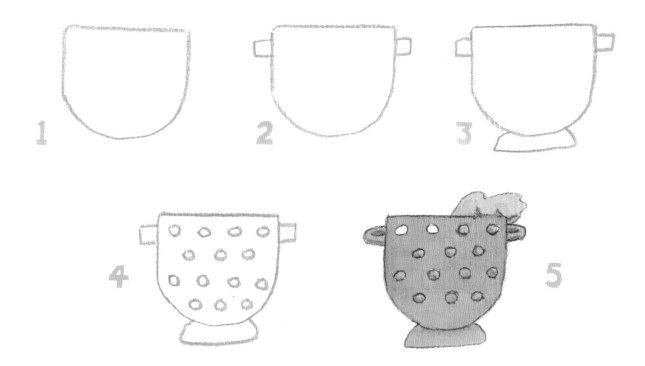

And now in 6 steps

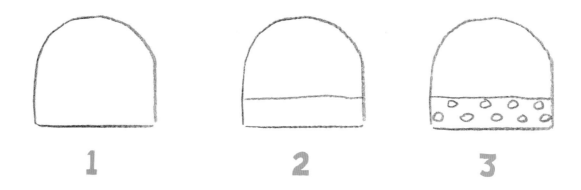

1   2   3

A big straw hat

4   5   6

Turn it again!

 1

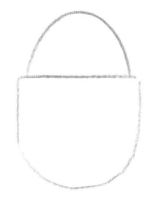 2

An egg cup

 3

 4

 5

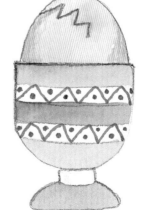 6

A teapot

Turn it again... Are you getting dizzy?

can you think of other objects with handles?

An octopus

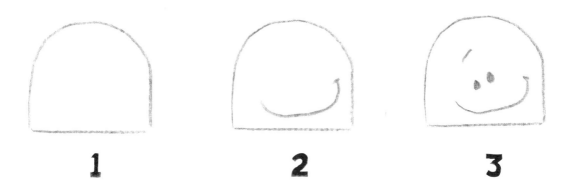

1 **2** **3**

There are other animals with lots of tentacles
you can draw... Can you think of any?

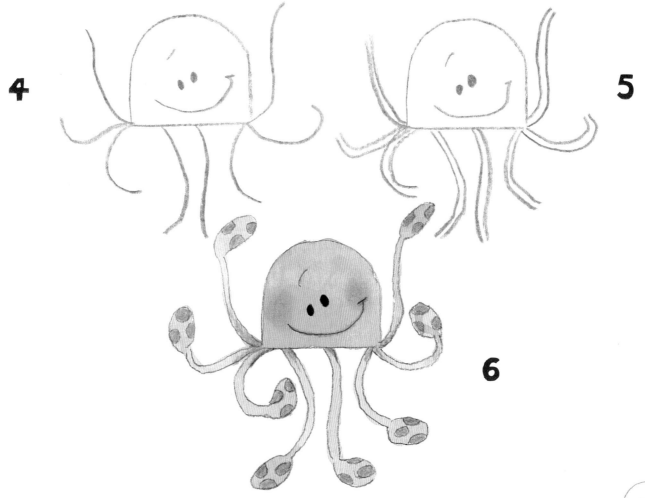

4 **5**

6

An egg-laying hen

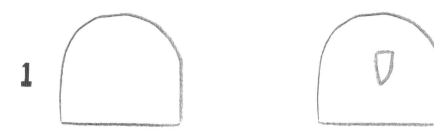

Try it in 7 steps!

An elephant

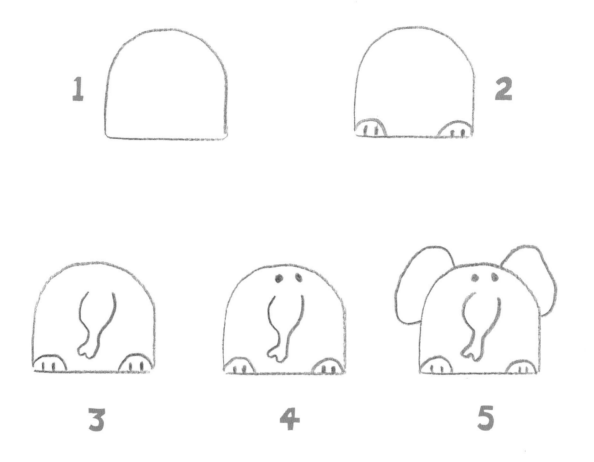

Can you draw the same elephant, but from the back?
We bet you can!

A bottle of perfume

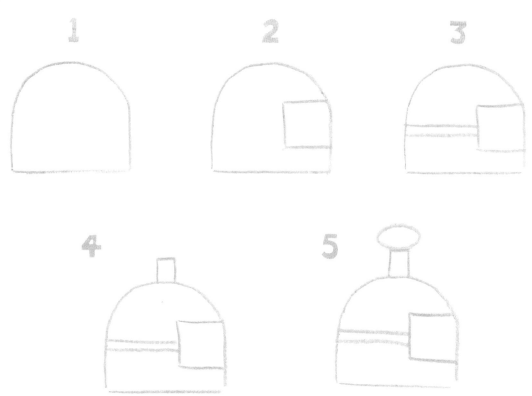

Don't forget the details!

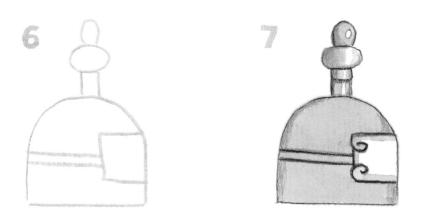

An owl

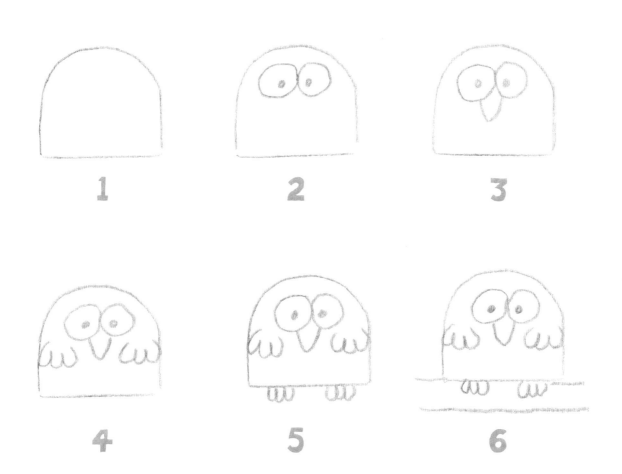

1

2

3

4

5

6

If you draw the wings outside the body shape, he'll look like he's about to take off flying.

7

Oval

A crab

1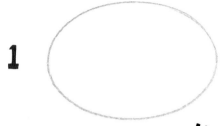

 2

How about in **6** steps?

3

 4

5

6

A sheep

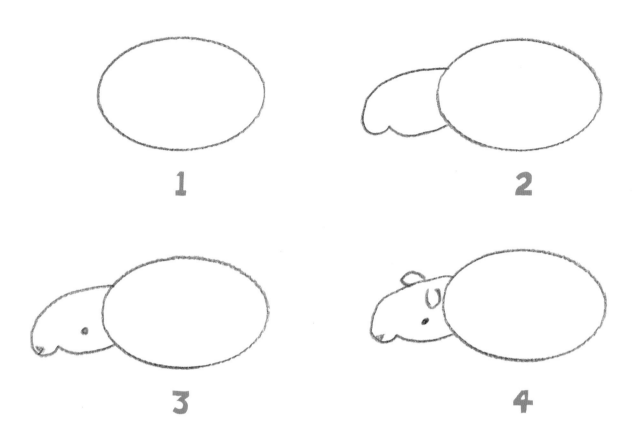

1 2 3 4

With this same oval shape, you can draw most four-legged animals you see on a farm.

5 6

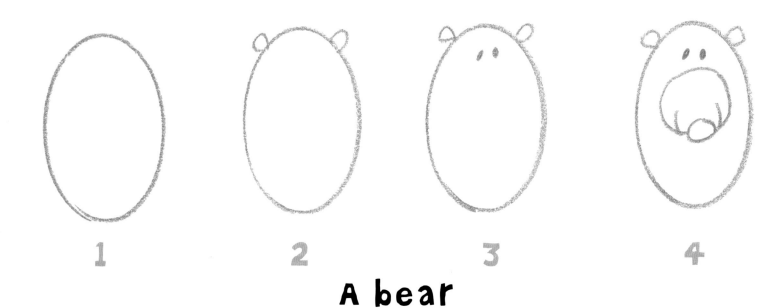

1   2   3   4

A bear

5   6   7

A hedgehog

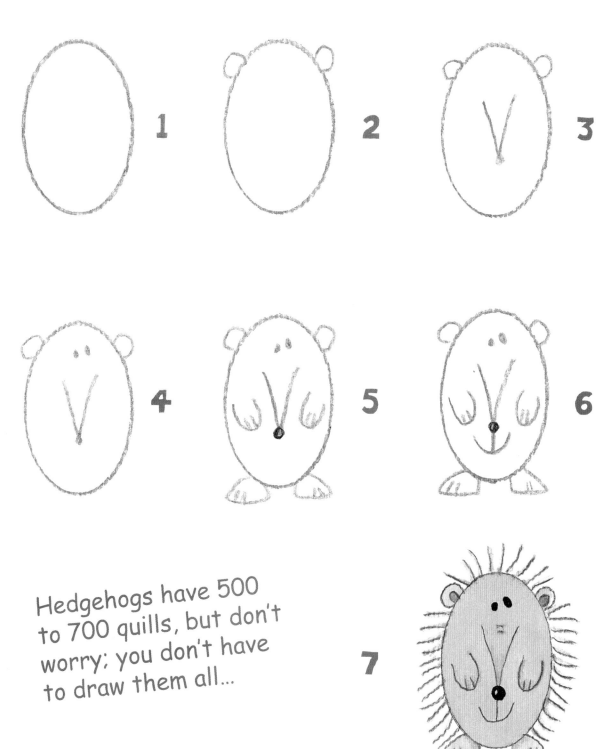

1

2

3

4

5

6

Hedgehogs have 500 to 700 quills, but don't worry; you don't have to draw them all...

7

A penguin

1

2

3

4

5

6

7

Add ice for the ground

1 **2** **3**

A parrot

4 **5** **6**

To draw your parrot from the side, just draw her beak on the side of her head. And one eye too, of course!

7

A turtle

1

2

Try it in 8 steps

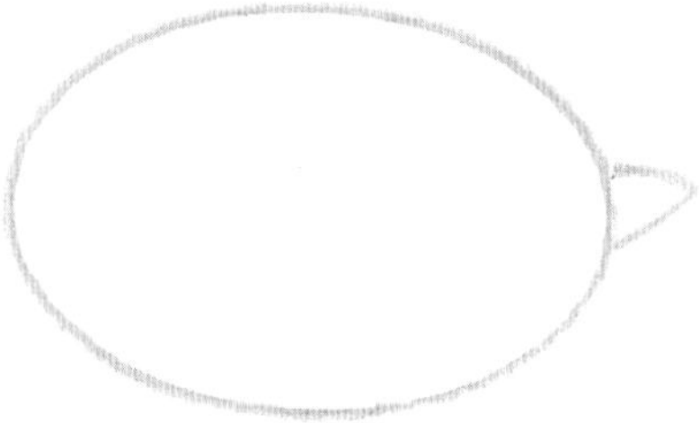

3

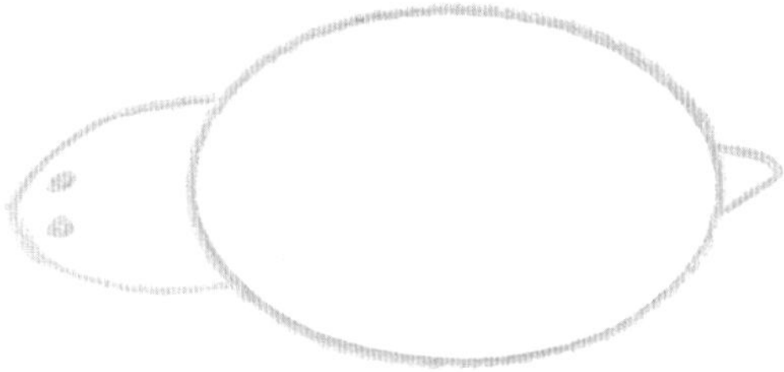

4

5

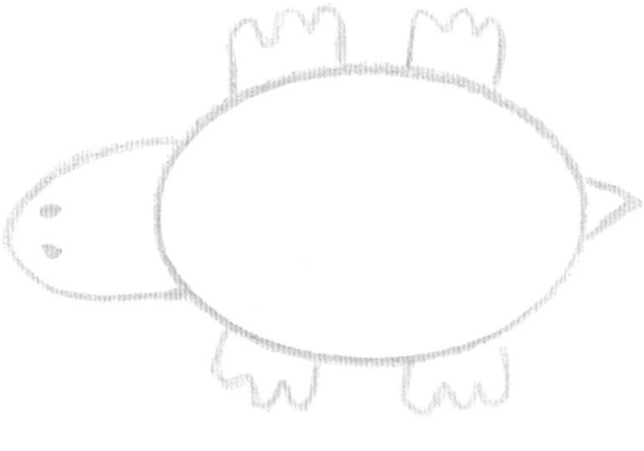

6

7

8

A mouse

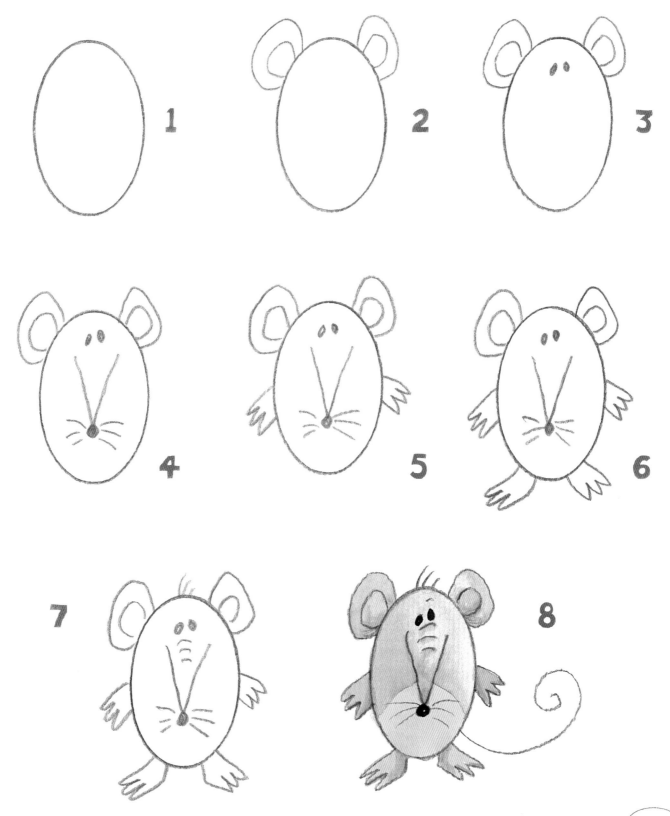

1

2

3

4

5

6

7

8

Equilateral triangle

A pyramid

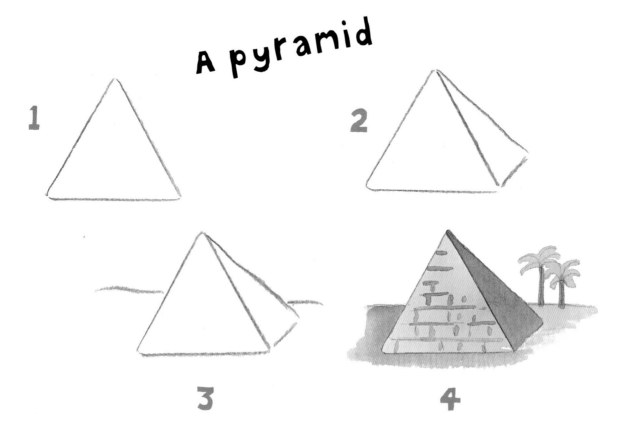

1
2
3
4

A pennant

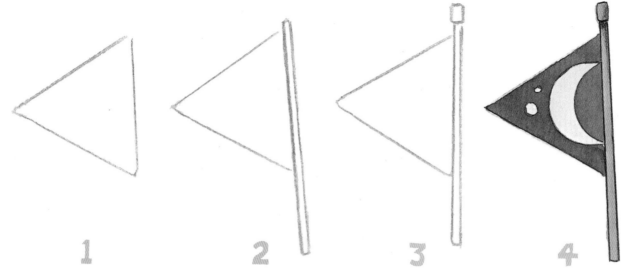

1
2
3
4

A teepee

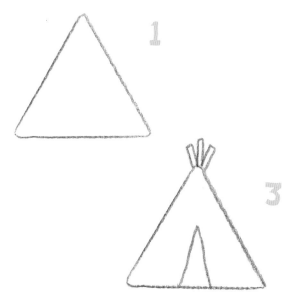

A tent

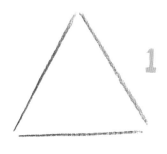
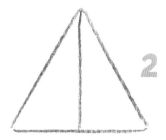
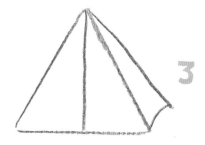
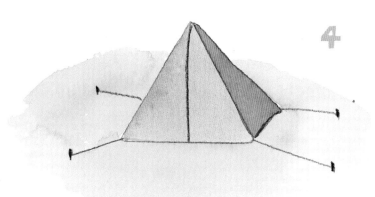

Turn it upside down!

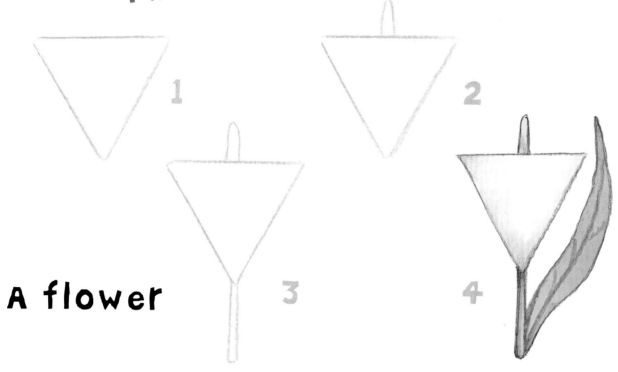

A flower

1 2 3 4

A cold soda

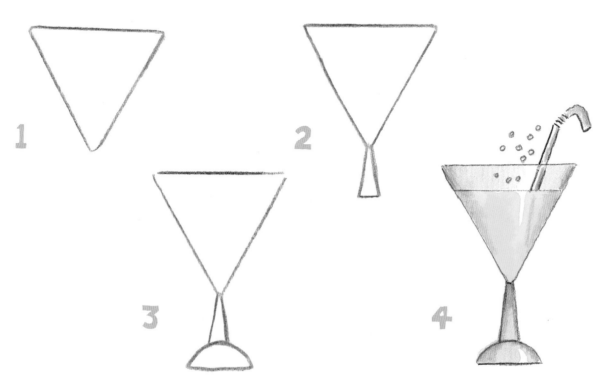

1 2 3 4

A triangle

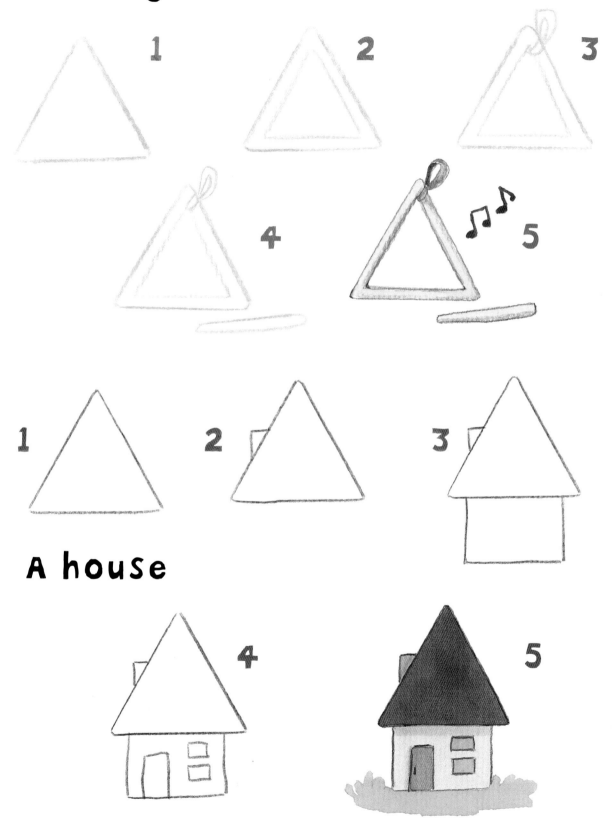

A house

Isosceles triangle

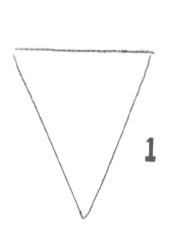

1

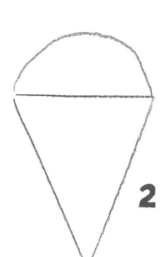

2

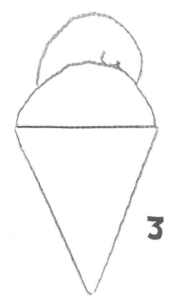

3

An ice cream cone

In just 6 steps

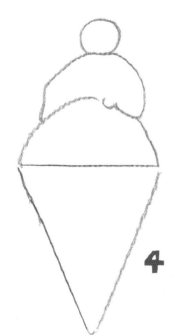

4

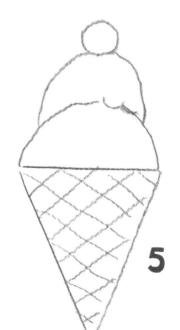

5

6

A rocket

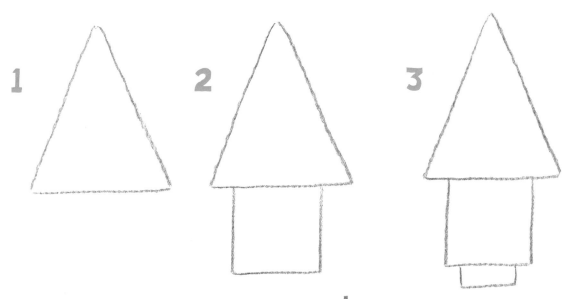

shooting into the sky

61

Looking right...

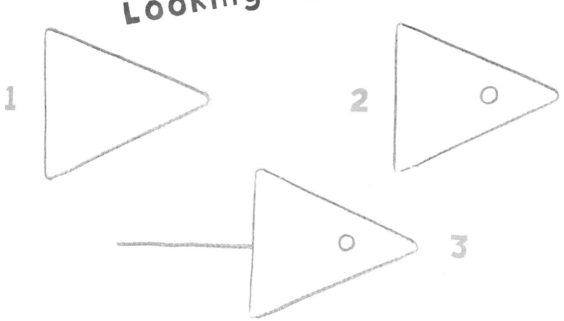

1
2
3

Fish bones

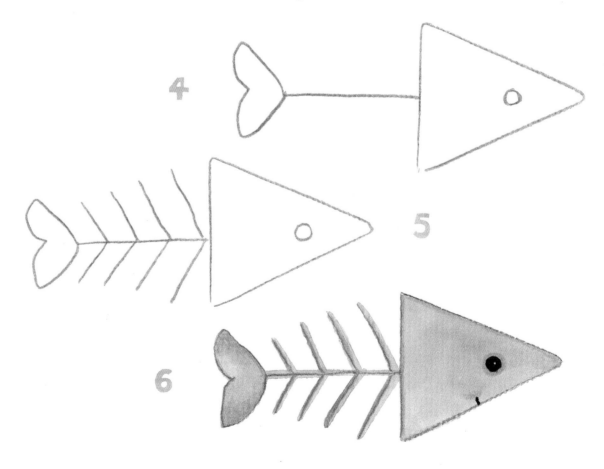

4
5
6

62

1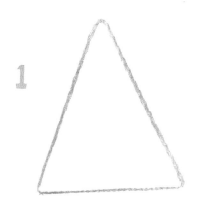

2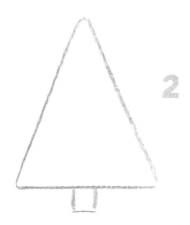

A Christmas tree

3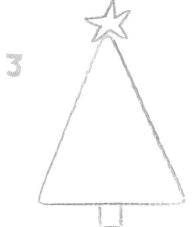

4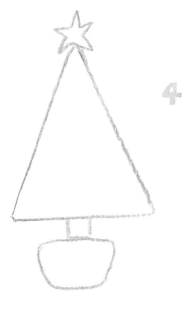

5

6

63

A wedge of cheese

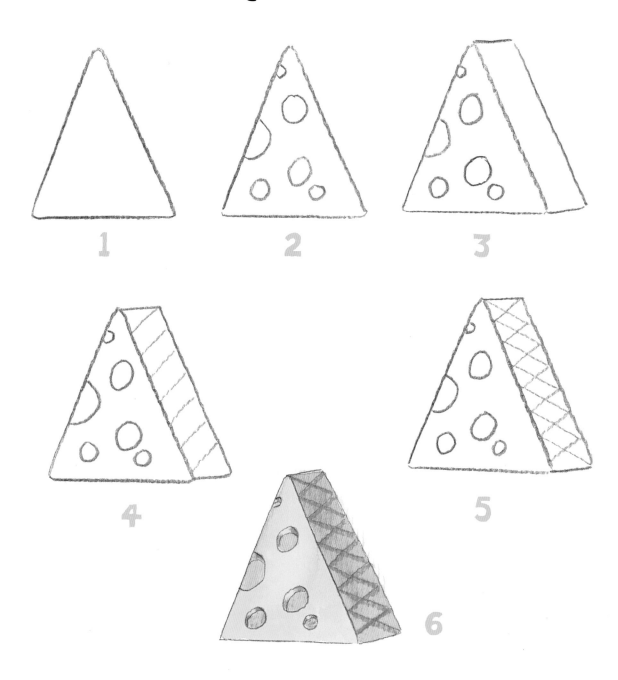

1

2

3

4

5

6

The holes help you make your cheese look different
than -for example- a slice of lemon pie.

1

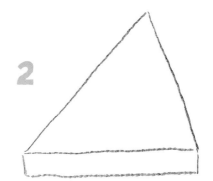

2

A sandwich

3

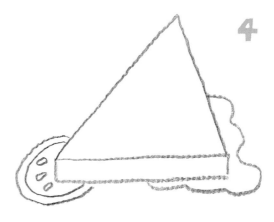

4

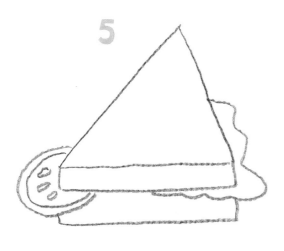

5

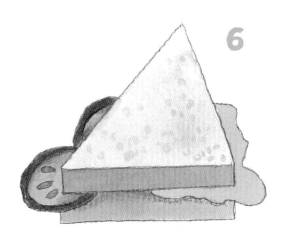

6

Square

 **1**
 **2**
 **3**

A note pad

 **4**
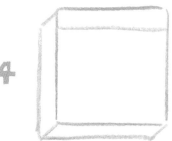 **5**

A present

 **1**
 **2**
 **3**

Make your wrapping paper special. Who is your present for?

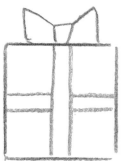 **4**
 **5**

66

A pot

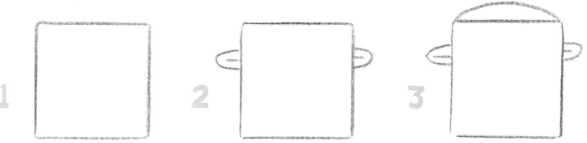

A coal car

A cardboard box

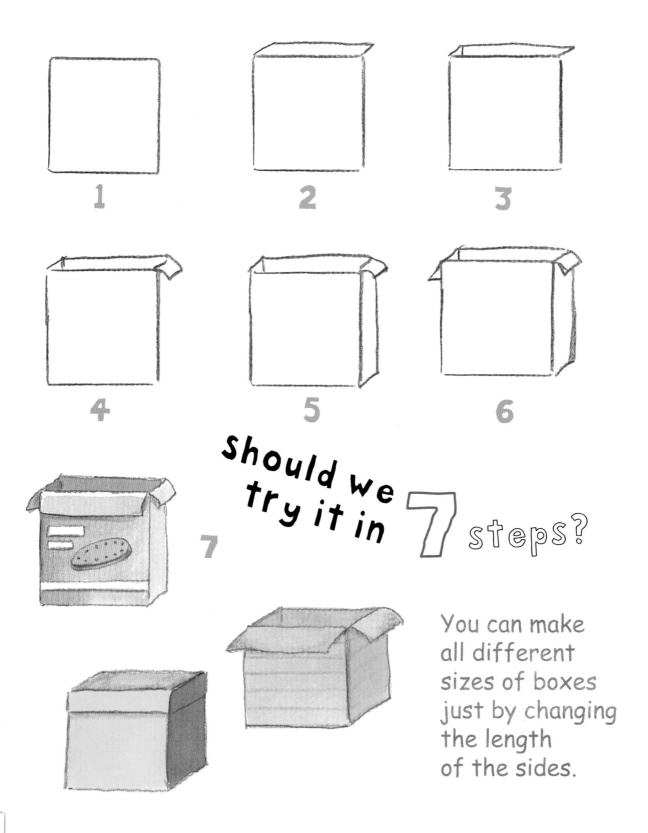

1

2

3

4

5

6

7

Should we try it in 7 steps?

You can make all different sizes of boxes just by changing the length of the sides.

A watering can

1

2

3

4

5

6

7

Add some flowers, using ovals and circles

A purse

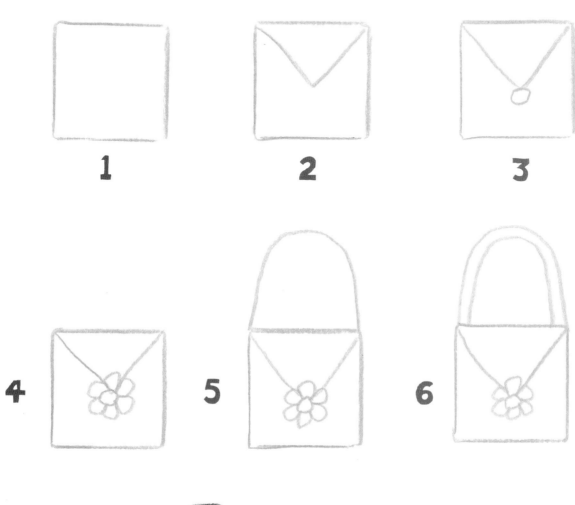

1

2

3

4

5

6

7

We joined three geometric shapes to make this purse. Can you see them all?

A jack-in-the-box

1

2

3

4

5

6

7

Did he scare you?

Rectangle

A birthday cake

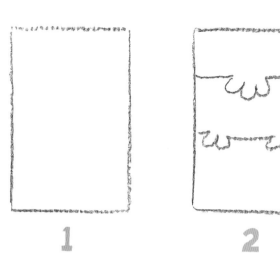 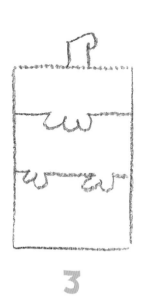 

1   2   3   4

An envelope

1   2

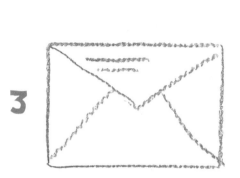 

3   4

A towel

And... half turn!

1

2

3

4

A train car

1

2

3

4

73

Let's go! 6 steps

A traffic light

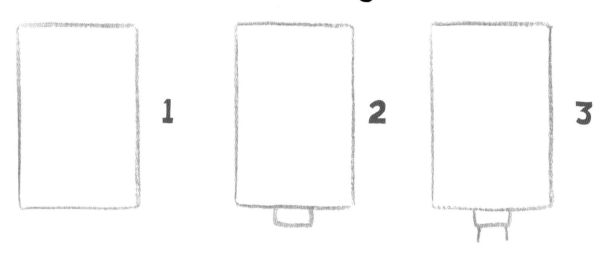

1   2   3

okay! Turn it again...

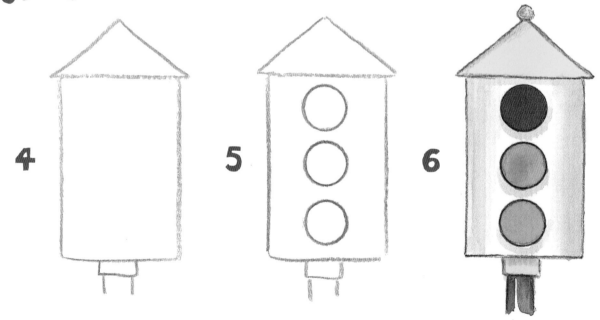

4   5   6

A building

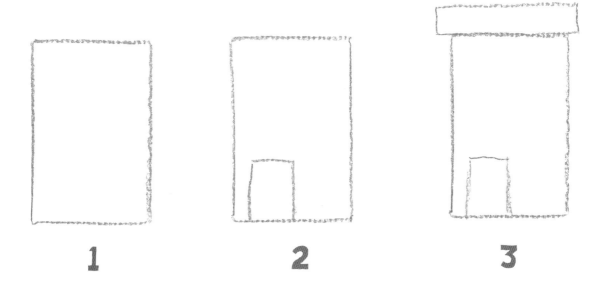

A few rectangles and squares are all you need
to construct your building.

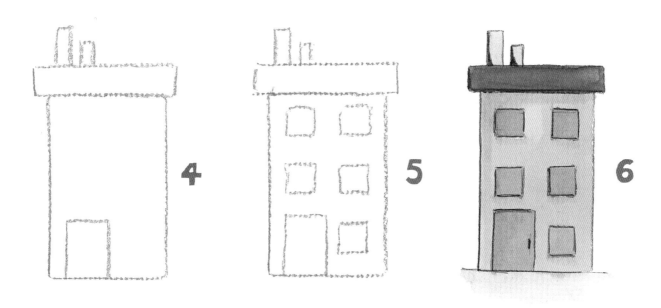

A reindeer

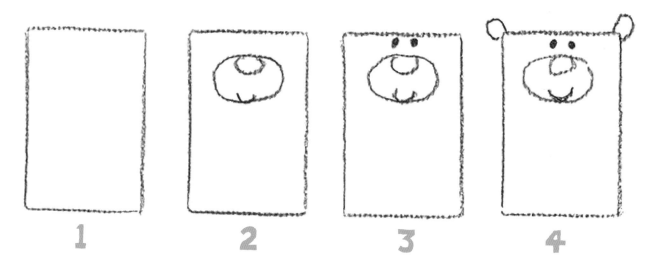

1   2   3   4

So easy in 7 steps

Be creative and try
drawing Santa's sleigh!

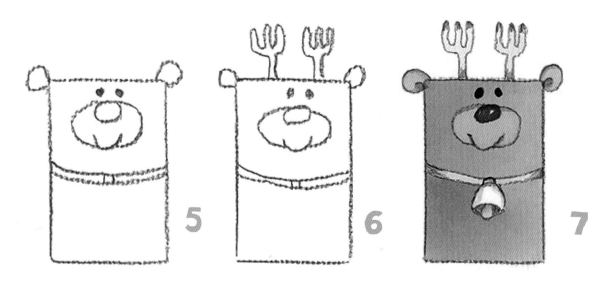

5   6   7

A tiger

With yellow construction paper and scissors,
you can make a really awesome greeting card.

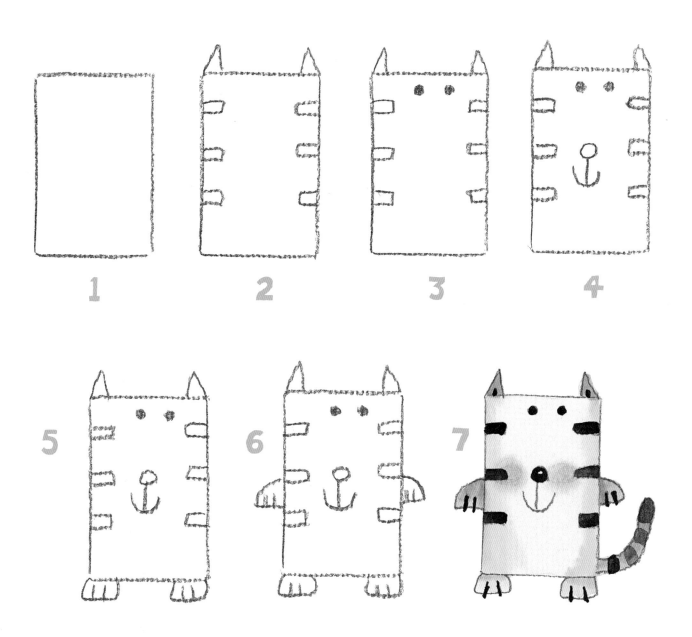

1   2   3   4

5   6   7

Trapezoid

A cupcake

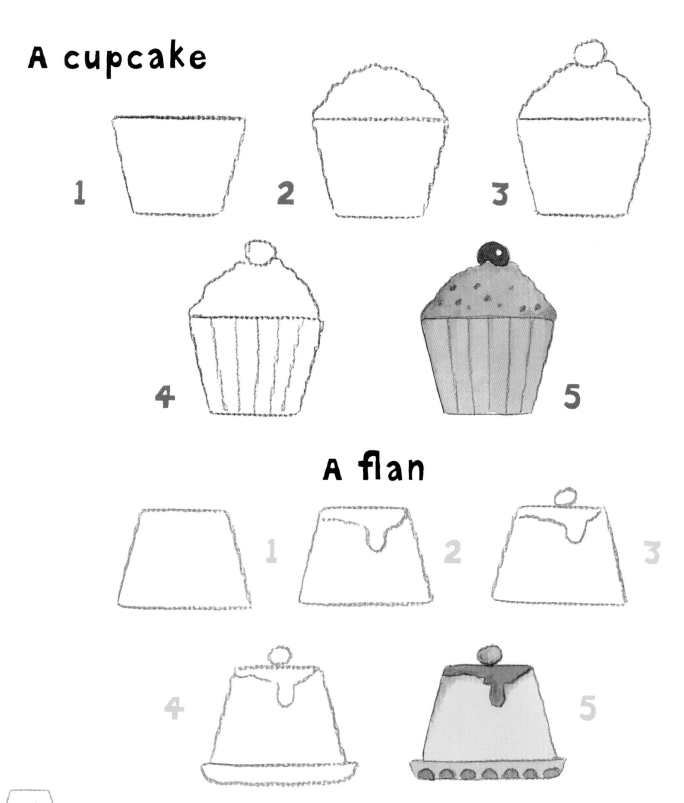

A flan

A candle

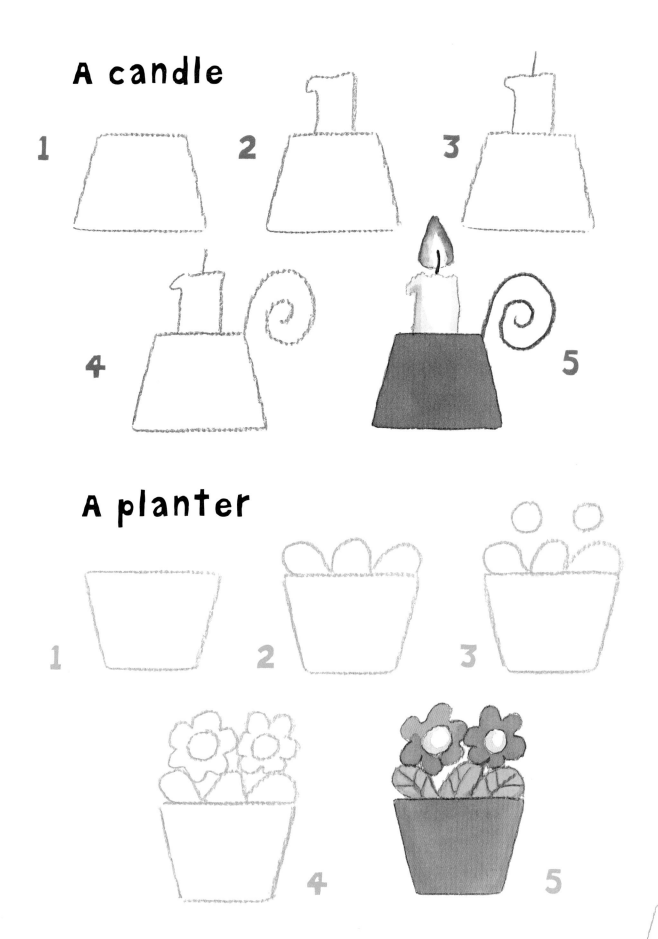

A planter

A tower

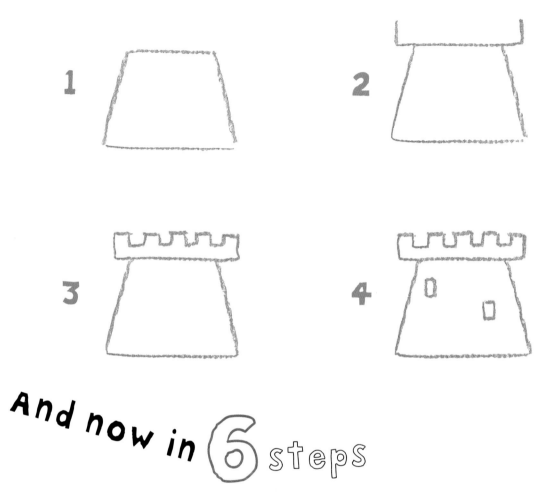

1

2

3

4

And now in 6 steps

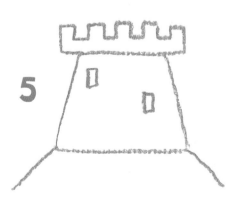

5

6

A bucket

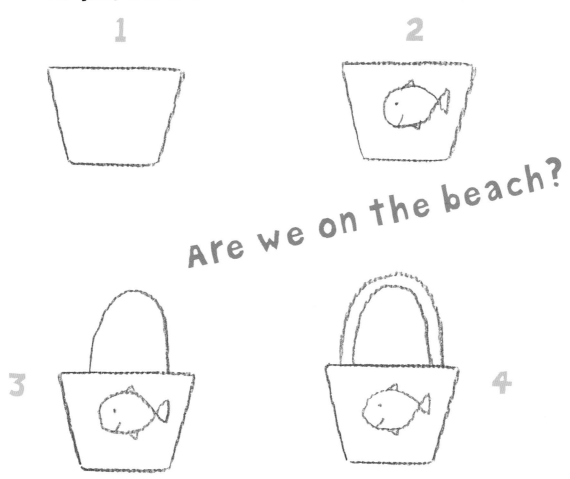

Are we on the beach?

Instead of a fish, you could draw a mushroom
on your bucket (page 8)... And where would you take
your bucket now?

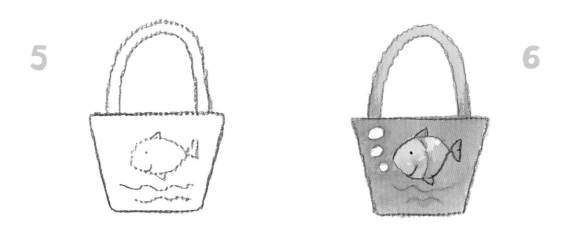

81

A shark

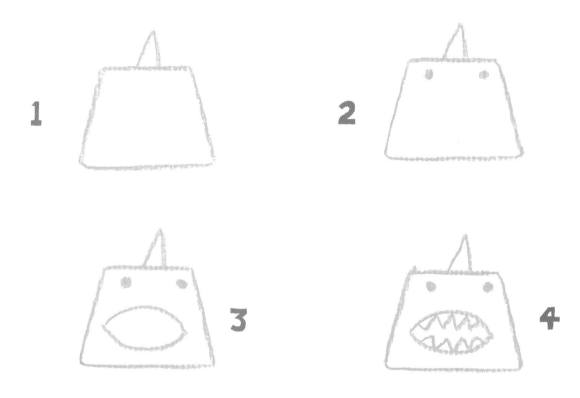

Don't be afraid!

A shovel

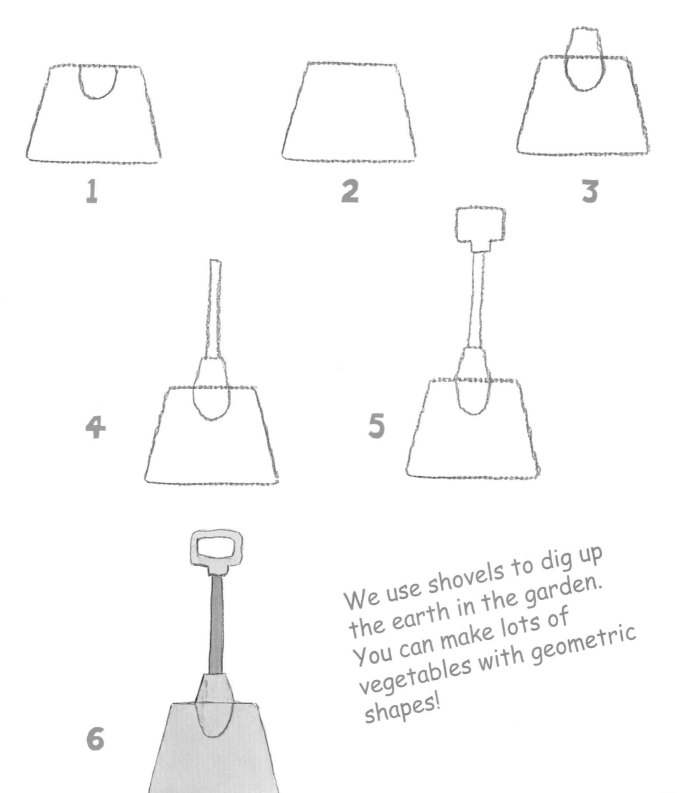

1

2

3

4

5

6

We use shovels to dig up the earth in the garden. You can make lots of vegetables with geometric shapes!

A boat

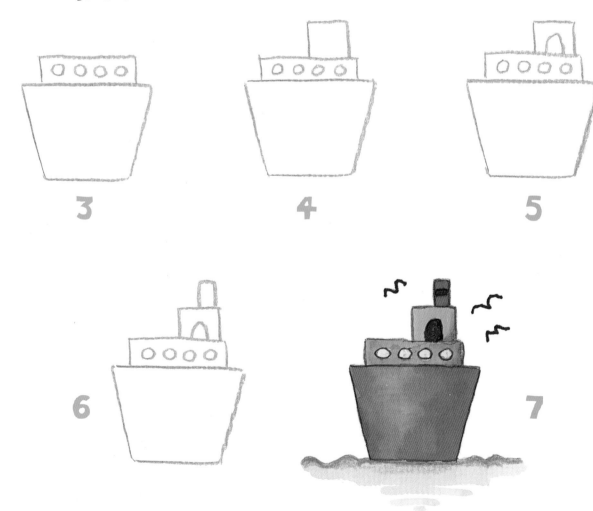

An inkpot

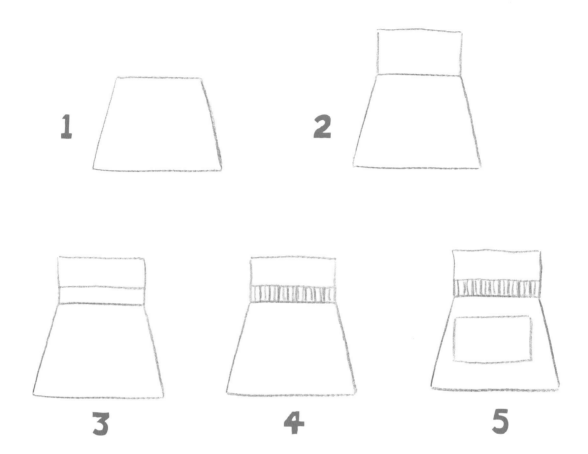

1   2   3   4   5

Go into your kitchen and look for pots and bottles and cans
with different shapes... We bet there are a lot!

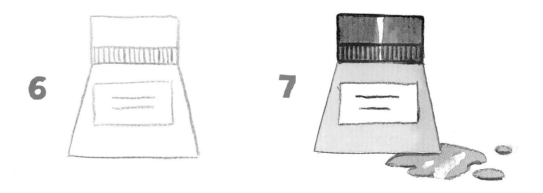

6   7

◯ Small circle

A radish

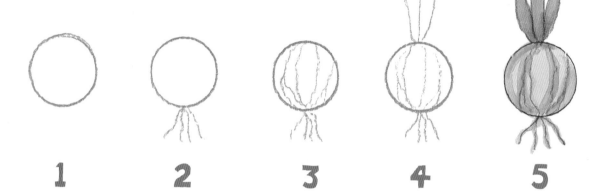

1   2   3   4   5

A lollipop

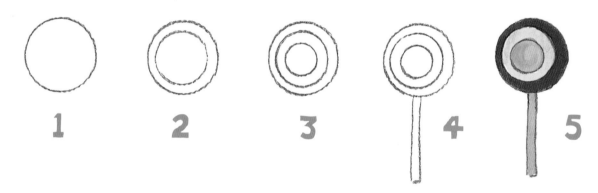

1   2   3   4   5

A ring

1   2   3   4   5

Bubbles

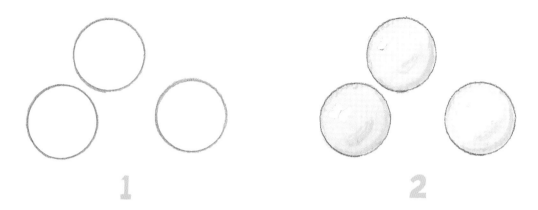

1   2

Tomatoes on the vine

1   2

A bunch of grapes

1   2

Rhomboid

A book

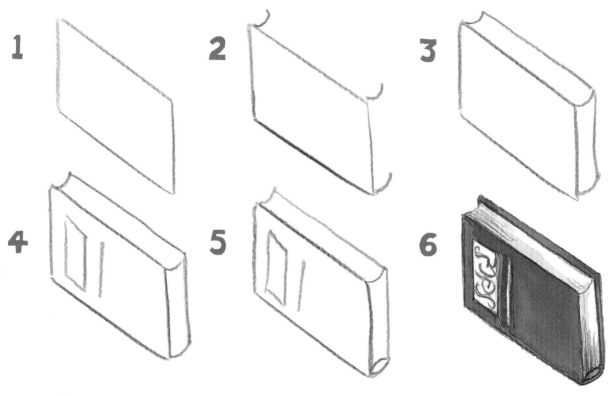

1
2
3
4
5
6

A domino

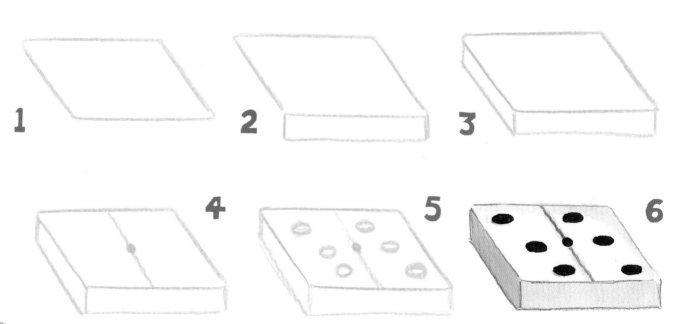

1
2
3
4
5
6

A box with a lid

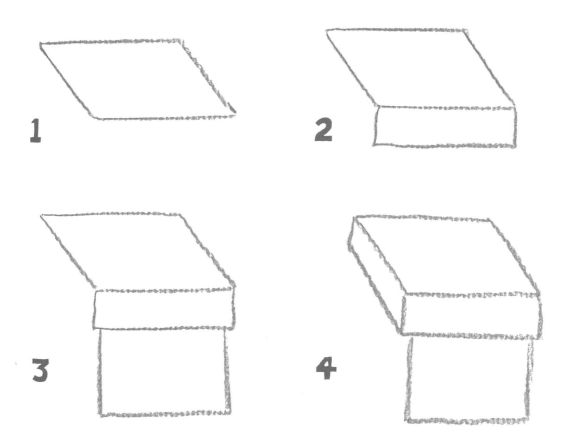

Practice perspective and you can learn to draw lots of the objects you see around you.

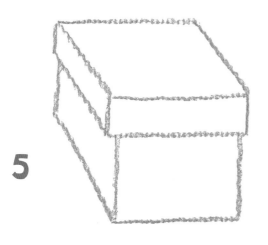

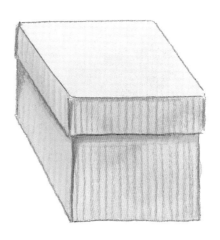

Hexagon and star

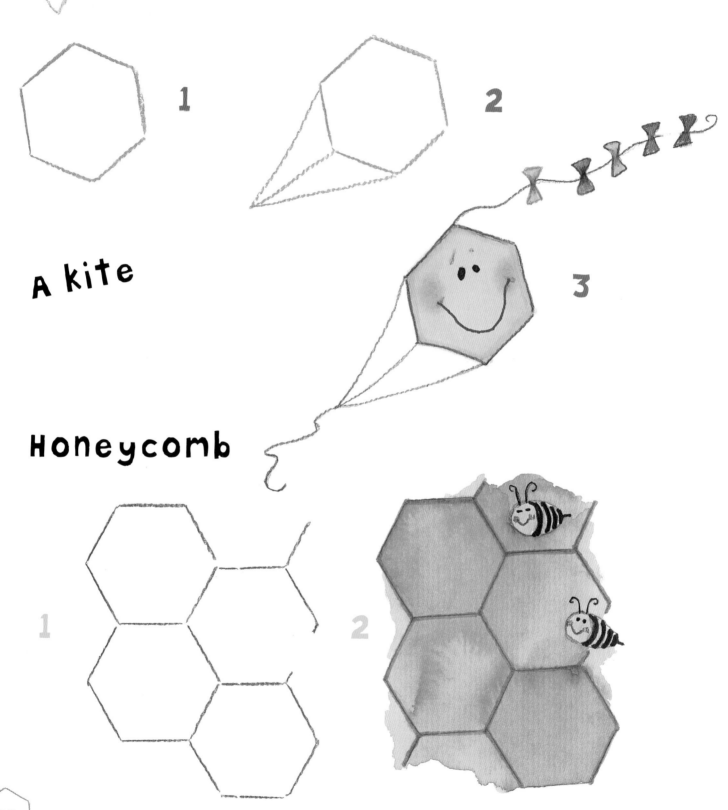

1

2

A kite

3

Honeycomb

1

2

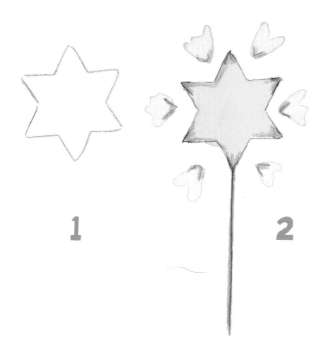

1   2

A magic wand

1

2

stars

If you make a background full of stars, you'll have drawn a piece of the Universe.

Combinations

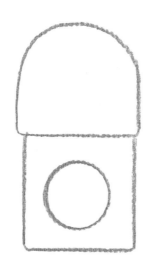

1

2

Funny robots

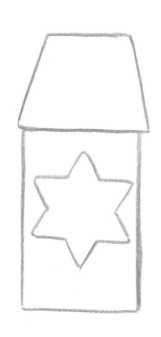

1

2

1

2

Why not try drawing a few robots by playing around with different shapes?

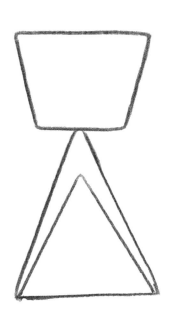

1

2

A bunch of ideas

Text and illustrations: **Rosa M. Curto**
Design and layout: **Estudi Guasch, S.L.**

© **Gemser Publications, S.L. 2015**
El Castell, 38   08329 Teià (Barcelona, Spain)
www.mercedesros.com

ISBN-13: 978-0-486-80221-3
ISBN-10: 0-486-80221-3
80221301   2015
Printed in China

This book is a co-publication of Gemser Publications, S.L., Barcelona, Spain, and Dover Publications, Inc., Mineola, New York.